The Columbus Academy
Reinberger Middle School Library
4300 Cherry Bottom Road
Gahanna, Ohio 43230

WITHDRAWN

W9-ASZ-425

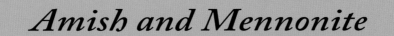

Amish and Mennonite

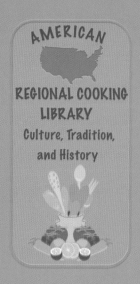

AMERICAN

REGIONAL COOKING
LIBRARY
Culture, Tradition,
and History

African American

American Indian

Amish and Mennonite

California

Hawaiian

Louisiana

Mexican American

Mid–Atlantic

Midwest

Northwest

New England

Southern

Southern Appalachian

Texas

Thanksgiving

Amish and Mennonite

Mason Crest Publishers

Philadelphia

Mason Crest Publishers Inc.
370 Reed Road
Broomall, Pennsylvania 19008
(866) MCP-BOOK (toll free)
www.masoncrest.com

Copyright © 2005 by Mason Crest Publishers. All rights reserved. No
part of this publication may be reproduced or transmitted in any form
or by any means, electronic or mechanical, including photocopying,
recording, taping, or any information storage and retrieval system,
without permission from the publisher.

First printing
1 2 3 4 5 6 7 8 9 10

Library of Congress Cataloging-in-Publication Data

Amish and Mennonite cooking / [compiled by Joyce Libal].
    p. cm. — (American regional cooking library)
  Includes bibliographical references and index.
  ISBN 1-59084-612-5 — ISBN 1-59084-609-5 (series)
  1. Cookery, Amish—United States—Juvenile literature. 2. Cookery, Mennonite—Juvenile
literature. 3. Amish—Social life and customs—Juvenile literature. 4. Mennonites—Social life
and customs—Juvenile literature. I. Libal, Joyce. II. Title. III. Series.
  TX715.T385 2005
  641.5'66—dc22
                              2004010195
Compiled by Joyce Libal.
Recipes tested and prepared by Bonni Phelps.
Produced by Harding House Publishing Services, Inc., Vestal, New York.
Interior design by Dianne Hodack.
Cover design by Michelle Bouch.
Printed and bound in the Hashemite Kingdom of Jordan.

Contents

Introduction
by the Culinary Institute of America

Cooking is a dynamic profession, one that presents some of the greatest challenges and offers some of the greatest rewards. Since 1946, the Culinary Institute of America has provided aspiring and seasoned food service professionals with the knowledge and skills needed to become leaders and innovators in this industry.

Here at the CIA, we teach our students the fundamental culinary techniques they need to build a sound foundation for their food service careers. There is always another level of perfection for them to achieve and another skill to master. Our rigorous curriculum provides them with a springboard to continued growth and success.

Food is far more than simply sustenance or the source of energy to fuel you and your family through life's daily regimen. It conjures memories throughout life, summoning up the smell, taste, and flavor of simpler times. Cooking is more than an art and a science; it provides family history. Food prepared with care epitomizes the love, devotion, and culinary delights that you offer to your friends and family.

A cuisine provides a way to express and establish customs—the way a food should taste and the flavors and aromas associated with that food. Cuisines are more than just a collection of ingredients, cooking utensils, and dishes from a geographic location; they are elements that are critical to establishing a culinary identity.

When you can accurately read a recipe, you can trace a variety of influences by observing which ingredients are selected and also by noting the technique that is used. If you research the historical origins of a recipe, you may find ingredients that traveled from East to West or from the New World to the Old. Traditional methods of cooking a dish may have changed with the times or to meet special challenges.

The history of cooking illustrates the significance of innovation and the trading or sharing of ingredients and tools between societies. Although the various cooking vessels over the years have changed, the basic cooking methods have remained the same. Through adaptation, a recipe created years ago in a remote corner of the world could today be recognized by many throughout the globe.

When observing the customs of different societies, it becomes apparent that food brings people together. It is the common thread that we share and that we value. Regardless of the occasion, food is present to celebrate and to comfort. Through food we can experience other cultures and lands, learning the significance of particular ingredients and cooking techniques.

As you begin your journey through the culinary arts, keep in mind the power that food and cuisine holds. When passed from generation to generation, family heritage and traditions remain strong. Become familiar with the dishes your family has enjoyed through the years and play a role in keeping them alive. Don't be afraid to embellish recipes along the way – creativity is what cooking is all about.

Amish and Mennonite Culture, History, and Traditions

Amish and Mennonite people have a shared history that stretches back to Europe and the time of the Protestant Reformation, when there were disagreements among Christians regarding specific religious beliefs. In 1525, one group, calling itself Anabaptists, was established in Switzerland. Adult baptism was a critical belief for the Anabaptists, and they lived somewhat apart from the mainstream of European life of the time. They did not incur debt, and they did not involve themselves in politics or war.

Later, some members broke away from the Anabaptists. One of these groups, under the leadership of a former Dutch priest named Menno Simons, called itself Mennonites. Simons believed people should maintain a plain way of living that included very simple dress and speech.

When William Penn, a Quaker, established a colony in Pennsylvania, one of his goals was to develop the area as a place where people could live in religious freedom. William Penn knew of Mennonites living in Germany, and he believed their farming ability would enhance the Pennsylvania colony and help ensure its survival and prosperity. He offered the Mennonites land for only ten cents per acre.

Mennonites began arriving and establishing farming communities in Pennsylvania in 1688. Other Mennonites immigrated to Russia. Toward the end of the 1800s and beginning of the 1900s, when they were forced out of Russia, many immigrated to the western part of the United States.

Meanwhile, back in Europe in the seventeenth century, Mennonites were further dividing over certain religious issues. One Swiss Mennonite elder named Jacob Amman disagreed with the number of times members received communion each year and the manner in which the concept of *meidung* (shunning) was carried out. In 1693, Jacob Amman and his followers broke with the Mennonite faith and established the Amish religion. Amman obtained additional followers in Switzerland and France, where they took up residence. The group flourished for a time, but eventually religious intolerance caused them to look for a new home. After moving to various parts of

France and Germany, they migrated to the new colonies in North America. Land in Pennsylvania was abundant, and beginning in the early 1700s, Amish people were able to establish communities where they lived with religious freedom.

Today, members of the Amish faith are friendly but maintain a closed society. They do not have a ministry that preaches outside of their own community, nor do they strive to convert others. Mennonites, on the other hand, operate the Mennonite Central Committee and Mennonite Board of Missions, through which they serve people in many different countries. Mennonites now number approximately one million, including Asians, African Americans, and Hispanic people. They have churches in South America, Africa, and Asia, as well as in Europe and North America.

Although Pennsylvania was their original destination, Amish people now live in more than twenty states and Canada. In Pennsylvania, members of the Amish community are often called "Pennsylvania Dutch." In this case, the word "Dutch" is a corruption of the word "Deutsch," which means German. Members of the Amish community sometimes refer to people who are not Amish as "English."

Amish people do not use electricity. They travel by horse and buggy; because of the animal's association with the military, horses are not ridden. Neither Amish nor Mennonite people serve in the armed forces; they are conscientious objectors.

Joy of family life is one of the many things that Amish and Mennonite people have in common. Large families, farming, and good home-cooked food are central to Old Order Mennonite and Amish life. As you page through this book, you may notice some recipes that are familiar to you. Most of the first immigrants to North American shores turned to farming as a means of survival. The same basic foods were available to everyone and became part of many cultural food traditions. Among Amish and Mennonite families, many women have been handing down and making the same recipes for decades. New recipes are obtained from farm magazines and newspapers and then shared with friends. While old recipes that feature expected ingredients such as apples and sauerkraut are still served, many foods that are currently enjoying widespread appeal, such as salsa, are also made. In this book you'll find a blend of the recipes that have been handed down for generations, and newer recipes that have become favorites in Amish and Mennonite families.

Before you cook...

If you haven't done much cooking before, you may find recipe books a little confusing. Certain words and terms can seem unfamiliar. You may find the measurements difficult to understand. What appears to be an easy or familiar dish may contain ingredients you've never heard of before. You might not understand what utensil the recipe calls for you to use, or you might not be sure what the recipe is asking you to do.

Reading the pages in this section before you get started may help you understand the directions better so that your cooking goes more smoothly. You can also refer back to these pages whenever you run into questions.

Safety Tips

Cooking involves handling very hot and very sharp objects, so being careful is common sense. What's more, you want to be certain that anything you plan on putting in your mouth is safe to eat. If you follow these easy tips, you should find that cooking can be both fun and safe.

Before you cook...

- Always wash your hands before and after handling food. This is particularly important after you handle raw meats, poultry, and eggs, as bacteria called salmonella can live on these uncooked foods. You can't see or smell salmonella, but these germs can make you or anyone who swallows them very sick.
- Make a habit of using potholders or oven mitts whenever you handle pots and pans from the oven or microwave.
- Always set pots, pans, and knives with their handles away from counter edges. This way you won't risk catching your sleeves on them—and any younger children in the house won't be in danger of grabbing something hot or sharp.
- Don't leave perishable food sitting out of the refrigerator for more than an hour or two.
- Wash all raw fruits and vegetables to remove dirt and chemicals.
- Use a cutting board when chopping vegetables or fruit, and always cut away from yourself.
- Don't overheat grease or oil—but if grease or oil does catch fire, don't try to extinguish the flames with water. Instead, throw baking soda or salt on the fire to put it out. Turn all stove burners off.
- If you burn yourself, immediately put the burn under cold water, as this will prevent the burn from becoming more painful.
- Never put metal dishes or utensils in the microwave. Use only microwave-proof dishes.
- Wash cutting boards and knives thoroughly after cutting meat, fish or poultry — especially when raw and before using the same tools to prepare other foods such as vegetables and cheese. This will prevent the spread of bacteria such as salmonella.
- Keep your hands away from any moving parts of appliances, such as mixers.
- Unplug any appliance, such as a mixer, blender, or food processor before assembling for use or disassembling after use.

Metric Conversion Table

Most cooks in the United States use measuring containers based on an eight-ounce cup, a teaspoon, and a tablespoon. Meanwhile, cooks in Canada and Europe are more apt to use metric measurements. The recipes in this book use cups, teaspoons, and tablespoons—but you can convert these measurements to metric by using the table below.

Temperature
To convert Fahrenheit degrees to Celsius, subtract 32 and multiply by .56.

212°F = 100°C
(this is the boiling point of water)
250°F = 110°C
275°F = 135°C
300°F = 150°C
325°F = 160°C
350°F = 180°C
375°F = 190°C
400°F = 200°C

Liquid Measurements
1 teaspoon = 5 milliliters
1 tablespoon = 15 milliliters
1 fluid ounce = 30 milliliters
1 cup = 240 milliliters
1 pint = 480 milliliters
1 quart = 0.95 liters
1 gallon = 3.8 liters

Measurements of Mass or Weight
1 ounce = 28 grams
8 ounces = 227 grams
1 pound (16 ounces) = 0.45 kilograms
2.2 pounds = 1 kilogram

Measurements of Length
¼ inch = 0.6 centimeters
½ inch = 1.25 centimeters
1 inch = 2.5 centimeters

Pan Sizes

Baking pans are usually made in standard sizes. The pans used in the United States are roughly equivalent to the following metric pans:

9-inch cake pan = 23-centimeter pan
11x7-inch baking pan = 28x18-centimeter baking pan
13x9-inch baking pan = 32.5x23-centimeter baking pan
9x5-inch loaf pan = 23x13-centimeter loaf pan
2-quart casserole = 2-liter casserole

Useful Tools, Utensils, Dishes

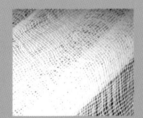
cheesecloth

cheese grater

Dutch oven

flour sifter

lemon juicer

loaf pans

pastry blender

roasting pan

rolling pin   stockpot   whisk

colander   wooden breadboard

Cooking Glossary

cream A term used to describe mixing sugar with butter or shortening until they are light and well blended.

cut Mix solid shortening or butter into flour, usually by using a pastry blender or two knives and making short, chopping stokes until the mixture looks like small pellets.

dash A very small amount, just a couple of drops.

diced Cut into small cubes or pieces.

dollop A small mound, about 1 or 2 tablespoons.

knead To work dough with the hands, lifting the far edge, placing it upon the rest, and pushing with the heal of the hands.

mince Cut into very small pieces.

set When a food preparation has completed the thickening process and can be sliced.

simmer Gently boiling, so that the surface of the liquid just ripples.

toss Turn food over quickly and lightly so that it is evenly covered with a liquid or powder.

whisk Stir briskly with a wire whisk.

zest A piece of the peel or the thin outer skin of an orange or lemon used as flavoring.

Special Amish and Mennonite Flavors

cheese

cinnamon

cloves

ginger

lemons

nutmeg

sauerkraut

vinegar

Amish and Mennonite Recipes

Baked Oatmeal

Pancakes, porridges, eggs, coffee cakes, bread, and fruit preserves are all part of traditional Mennonite and Amish breakfasts. This delicious cereal can be made the night before, and popped in the oven in the morning.

Ingredients:

2 eggs
1½ teaspoons vanilla
¾ cup brown sugar, packed
1½ teaspoons baking powder
1 teaspoon nutmeg
¼ teaspoon salt
⅓ cup butter
1¼ cups milk
3 cups uncooked oatmeal (quick-cooking variety)
milk or light cream (half and half)

Cooking utensils you'll need:
measuring cups
measuring spoons
mixing bowl
whisk
small saucepan
baking dish
plastic wrap

Directions:

Whisk eggs with vanilla, and stir in brown sugar, baking powder, nutmeg, and salt. Melt butter in saucepan and stir in 1¼ cups milk. Stir milk mixture into egg mixture. Stir in uncooked oatmeal, pour into buttered baking dish, cover with plastic wrap, and refrigerate. The next morning, remove plastic wrap, and bake oatmeal at 350° Fahrenheit for 35 to 45 minutes (until lightly browned along the edges and *set* in the center). Serve with milk or light cream.

Amish and Mennonite Culture

Historically, Amish people were sometimes called *Häftler*, which means "hooks and eyes," while Mennonites were called "button people," *Knöpfler*. Today most Mennonites dress modestly but in modern styles. Some conservative Mennonite groups require women to cover their heads, but many allow women to wear slacks, and some even permit shorts in the summer. Amish styles have remained basically the same since the eighteenth century, although there are style variations in different areas of the country. Amish men grow beards after they marry. At one time men were not allowed to trim their beards, but today, young men do sometimes trim them. Interestingly, they never have mustaches. This is because the group decided to shave off their mustaches in the 1800s to protest war. At that time many soldiers had mustaches.

Pumpkin Pancakes

Preheat pancake griddle. (See "Tips.")

Ingredients:

1 cup flour
⅛ teaspoon baking soda
⅛ teaspoon baking powder
2 tablespoons sugar
¼ teaspoon cinnamon
⅛ teaspoon ginger

⅛ teaspoon nutmeg
1 egg
1¼ cups milk
2 tablespoons melted butter
½ cup cooked or canned pumpkin

Cooking utensils you'll need:
measuring cups
measuring spoons
2 mixing bowls
metal spatula
wire whisk
pancake griddle

Directions:

Mix the dry ingredients in one bowl. *Whisk* the eggs and remaining ingredients in the second bowl. Pour the wet mixture into the dry mixture, and stir. Use the ¼ measuring cup to pour small amounts of batter onto the hot griddle, and cook each side until done. You'll have about 20 small pancakes.

Tips:

These pancakes are delicious served with apple butter and a *dollop* of sour cream.

It is not usually necessary to use cooking oil or vegetable spray when frying the pancakes on a griddle or in a nonstick skillet.

To know if your pancake griddle is hot enough to begin frying the pancakes, carefully throw a couple drops of water on the griddle's surface. If it quickly sizzles, pops, and evaporates, it's time to start cooking.

Amish and Mennonite Food History

American Indians were roasting pieces of pumpkin over open fires before the first Amish and Mennonite immigrants arrived in North America. The food probably originated in Mexico as seeds from similar plants dating to 7000 B.C. have been discovered there. Pumpkins are one of the larger vegetables, and when they are ripening or in storage, they can be utilized in several different ways, from pancakes for breakfast to cookies and pies for dessert.

Breakfast Pizza

Eggs and sausage feature prominently in Amish and Mennonite breakfasts as they do in many cultures. Like busy moms everywhere, these cooks appreciate meals that are quick and easy to make, especially in the early morning hours. Women cook new recipes they get from friends or read on prepared food packages purchased at grocery stores. That may be how they came to make this dish. You can bake this pizza ahead of time, heat a slice in the microwave, and take it with you as you rush to catch the school bus.

Preheat oven to 375° Fahrenheit.

Ingredients:

one pre-baked pizza shell (see "Tip")
1 pound mild bulk sausage
1 cup shredded potatoes (or frozen hash browns, thawed)
1 cup shredded cheddar cheese
5 eggs
¼ cup milk
salt and pepper
2 tablespoons shredded Parmesan cheese

Cooking utensils you'll need:
skillet
measuring cups
measuring spoon
mixing bowl
whisk
pizza pan or jelly roll pan

Directions:

Cook sausage in skillet until well browned, drain, and place on pizza crust. Layer potatoes on sausage followed by cheddar cheese. *Whisk* eggs with milk and a few shakes of salt and pepper, and pour on pizza. Top with Parmesan cheese, and bake 30 minutes.

Tip:

If you would like to make your own pizza shell, here's an easy recipe: Put 1½ cups of very warm water in a large mixing bowl, and sprinkle one package of active dry yeast over it. Stir to dissolve the yeast, and then stir in 1 of cup flour and ½ teaspoon salt. Stir in 2½ additional cups flour. Use your hands to *knead* the dough, adding up to ½ cup of additional flour, as necessary. (Be careful to not add too much flour as it can make the pizza dough stiff and dry.) Rub a little olive oil around in the bowl, place the dough in the bowl, swirl it around to cover the bottom with oil, and turn it upside down so the oiled surface is on top. Cover the bowl with a clean towel, and set it somewhere warm for about an hour. Then oil the cookie sheet or pizza pan, use your hand to punch the dough down, and spread it in the pan. Bake the dough for 10 or 15 minutes at 450° Fahrenheit, and then proceed with the Breakfast Pizza recipe. To make your pizza shell more nutritious, substitute 1 cup of whole wheat flour for 1 cup of the white flour.

Amish Culture

The rejection of modern conveniences makes it challenging for Amish families to continue making a living from the family farm. Although many families maintain their rural lifestyle, growing their own vegetables and raising animals for food, many men have started small businesses such as cattle sales and carpentry. Other men and older boys hold jobs in lumber mills or factories. Women commonly sell baked goods or preserves or make extra money by sewing, weaving rugs, or selling flowers. Older girls sometimes work in restaurants.

Homemade Lemonade

Homemade lemonade is a favorite beverage among Mennonite and Amish families.

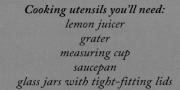

Ingredients:

3 lemons
2 cups water
2 cups sugar

Directions:

Wash the lemons, cut them in half, squeeze out the juice, remove and discard the seeds, and set the juice aside. Grate enough of the lemon peel to equal 1½ tablespoons of lemon *zest*, and put it in the saucepan. Stir in water and sugar, place over medium heat, *simmer* 5 minutes, cool, and strain through cheesecloth or wire strainer. Stir in lemon juice, and store in covered jars in refrigerator. To serve, place 2 tablespoons lemon syrup in each glass, and stir in ½ cup cold water and ice.

Cooking utensils you'll need:
lemon juicer
grater
measuring cup
saucepan
glass jars with tight-fitting lids

Tips:

To get more juice out of a lemon, use your hand to apply pressure to the lemon while rolling it back and forth on a hard surface before cutting.

For a spicy version of this lemonade, add a cinnamon stick to the saucepan when making the syrup.

Garnish individual servings with mint sprigs, if desired.

Amish Culture

Amish children are bilingual. A dialect of German is usually spoken in Amish homes, and children learn to read German as well as English.

Life for Amish young people is different from what it is like for other North American children and teens—and yet in some ways, it is not so different. Little girls play with homemade rag dolls called *lumba babba*, but these dolls do not have faces. Young children play in sandboxes and sometimes on trampolines. Fishing and iceskating are other favorite pastimes, and volleyball is a popular sport. Most Amish children attend one-room schools, where students in all grades are together, and formal schooling ends with the eighth grade. Sometimes Mennonite children attend public schools.

Indoor and outdoor chores take up much time on family farms. As early as age four, some children are beginning to learn small tasks. Girls generally help with cooking, baking, and gardening, while boys help with planting, cleaning the barn, feeding animals, etc., but girls often also do farm chores. Amish teens are not prohibited from going to shopping malls and movies, however, they are also not encouraged to do this, and many of them never attend such things.

Whether or not to become baptized and join the church is an individual decision, and pressure is not put upon children to choose the Amish life. People may remain unbaptized indefinitely, but they are then not allowed to marry. Few people choose this life. Ninety percent decide to be baptized, and most of the remaining 10 percent join a similar faith, such as Mennonite.

Chicken Pot Pie

This well-known dish takes different forms. In some areas, it is a thick stew made on top of the stove and includes large, freshly made noodles. Other cooks place a piecrust on top of the stew and bake it in the oven. Choose whichever method you like when making this dish.

Ingredients:

4 or 5 pounds chicken pieces
1 medium onion, chopped
1 celery stalk, chopped
1 bay leaf
8 cups water
4 potatoes, (cut in bite-sized pieces)
1 carrot, chopped
1 tablespoon parsley
½ cup each of any vegetables you like
  (peas, corn, green beans)
salt and pepper to taste
2 cups flour
¼ teaspoon salt
2 eggs
milk, sour cream, or heavy cream (whipping cream)

Cooking utensils you'll need:
stockpot
measuring cup
measuring spoon
pastry blender or 2 butter knives
mixing bowl
rolling pin
breadboard or other flat surface
baking dish (if using oven method)

Directions:

Put chicken, onion, celery, and bay leaf in stockpot with water, and *simmer* until chicken is tender. Remove bay leaf (discard) and chicken, cool, and cut meat from bones. Meanwhile put broth in refrigerator to cool, skim fat off surface and discard. Return meat to broth in pot. (If using oven method, measure broth. Use 2 cups in this recipe and save the rest for another purpose.) Add potatoes, carrots, any other vegetables you like, and parsley, *simmer* 20 minutes, and add salt and pepper to taste. (If using oven method, thicken broth by adding 2 tablespoons flour dissolved in ½ cup water.)

Meanwhile, mix 2 cups flour with ¼ teaspoon salt, and *cut* in eggs. Cut in milk, sour cream, or heavy cream 1 tablespoon at a time until dough is soft and holds together well. Sprinkle extra flour on board or other flat surface and rolling pin and roll out dough. For stovetop method: Cut dough into 1- or 2-inch squares, drop them into the simmering stew, and cook another 20 minutes. For oven method: Preheat oven to 400° Fahrenheit. Pour stew into baking dish, top with pie crust, crimp the edges, cut slits in the top, and bake for 20 minutes. Reduce heat to 375° Fahrenheit, and continue baking an additional 40 minutes (or until crust is browned).

Tip:

When using the oven method, instead of covering the entire surface of the stew with the pie crust, you can use cookie cutters to cut shapes and place them on the stew before baking. Place baking dish on a cookie sheet in case of spillover.

Amish Culture

Attending livestock and household auctions is a way to combine business and socializing. Another way to do this involves the ancient craft of quilting, which is both a necessity and a hobby for many Amish and Mennonite women. Being an art as well as a craft, quilting provides a way for women to display their sense of color and design. It allows women to gather for socializing since they often meet to complete the final quilting. This is another occasion for cooking and serving favorite foods and trying new recipes. For some women, quilting has become a business as many people admire and want to own authentic Amish or Mennonite quilts. It is also a way to earn money for community needs. Mennonites routinely hold quilt auctions to support overseas relief projects.

Sauerbraten

Much physical labor is necessary to run a successful farm, and noon meals (called "dinner" by the Amish) need to be substantial to replenish energy levels. For many families, it is the main meal of the day. This pot roast calls to mind the German heritage of Amish and Mennonite people. It takes 4 or 5 days to complete this recipe, so plan ahead!

Ingredients:

2 cups vinegar
4 whole cloves
4 bay leaves
12 peppercorns
4 pound rump, chuck, or round beef roast
1 tablespoon cooking oil
3 large onions
4 carrots
12 gingersnaps
1 tablespoon sugar
salt and pepper to taste

Cooking utensils you'll need:
measuring cup
measuring spoon
small bowl
large bowl
plastic wrap
Dutch oven

Directions:

Mix the vinegar, cloves, bay leaves, and peppercorns in the small bowl. Cover with plastic wrap, and place in the refrigerator for 3 or 4 days.

Wash the meat and pat it dry with paper towels, place the meat in the large bowl, pour the vinegar mixture over it, add water to cover the meat, cover the bowl with plastic wrap, and refrigerate until the next day.

Slice the onion, cut the carrots into chunks, and set them aside. Put the cooking oil and meat in the Dutch oven, place over medium heat, and cook, turning the meat as necessary to brown all sides. Strain the vinegar mixture to remove the spices. Add the onions, carrots, and 1 cup of the strained vinegar to the meat. (Put the remaining vinegar mixture in the refrigerator.) Cover the Dutch oven, place it over low heat, and cook for about 3 hours, adding more vinegar mixture as necessary. When the meat is cooked and tender, stir in the sugar. Crumble the gingersnaps and add them to the pot. Cover again, *simmer* for 10 minutes, and serve.

Amish Culture

Thanksgiving is an important holiday as is Christmas, which some Amish families celebrate on January 6 rather than December 25. Other important religious holidays include Good Friday and Easter. Amish and Mennonite children do color eggs and hunt for them on Easter morning. The Ascension and Pentecost are also important religious occasions.

"Frolics" is a word Amish people use to describe gatherings that occur for the purpose of work but that afford the opportunity to socialize with members of the community. Barn raisings and the joint harvesting of some crops constitute frolics.

Sister's days are days when married women get together with their sisters to socialize.

Salmon Croquettes

Canned salmon is a staple in many Mennonite and Amish kitchens and is used to make quick and easy main dishes like this one. Salmon contains important omega-3 fatty acids and is one of the most nutritious foods you can eat. It helps strengthen your bones and brain while lowering your risk for heart disease, dementia, and depression. It also helps pregnant women lower their risk for premature delivery. Health professionals suggest eating fish twice a week.

Ingredients:

2 tablespoons cooking oil
One 15-ounce can salmon
¾ cup saltine cracker crumbs (or ¾ cup dry bread crumbs and ¼ teaspoon salt)
2 tablespoons **minced** onion
2 tablespoons minced red or green bell pepper
¼ teaspoon pepper
1 tablespoon lemon juice (optional)
1 egg
3 tablespoons milk

Cooking utensils you'll need:
measuring cups
measuring spoons
mixing bowl
skillet

Directions:

Put cooking oil in skillet. Break up salmon, including bones and skin, in mixing bowl (do not drain). Mix in remaining ingredients, and use your hands to form mixture into patties. Fry on both sides in hot oil until well browned.

Tip:

To neatly crush crackers, place them in a heavy-duty plastic bag, and crush them with a rolling pin.

Amish and Mennonite Culture

"Old Order" is a term used to describe the most conservative Mennonite and Amish communities. Members of these communities strive to avoid vanity. Mirrors are usually absent from Amish homes, and when they do exist, they are often partially draped. Girls do not cut their hair, and most groups do not allow hair to be worn over the ears. Women usually wear their hair pulled back in a bun. The rules of the church that Amish live by are called *ordnung*. Amish adults do not like to have their photograph taken because the Bible cautions against "graven images of any likeness . . . that is not in heaven" (Exodus, chapter 20).

Roast Chicken with Chestnut Stuffing

The Amish usually refer to stuffing as "filling." Chicken is most often served in pieces and combined with other ingredients, such as filling, that stretch out the meat to serve more people. Roast chicken like this is a special meal.

Preheat oven to 475° Fahrenheit.

Ingredients:

½ pound chestnuts
¼ cup butter
¼ cup chopped celery
¼ cup chopped onion
½ teaspoon salt
1 teaspoons sage
½ teaspoon marjoram
¼ teaspoon savory

¼ teaspoon thyme
2 cups bread crumbs
1 egg, beaten
one 5–pound chicken
sprig of fresh sage, marjoram,
or thyme (optional)
salt and pepper
1 cup sour cream

Cooking utensils you'll need:
small, sharp knife
baking dish or jelly roll pan
large saucepan
small saucepan
measuring cups
measuring spoons
mixing bowl
meat thermometer
roasting pan

Directions:

Carefully cut an X on the flat side of each chestnut, place them in the baking dish, and bake for 15 minutes. Remove from oven, and reduce oven to 400° Fahrenheit. When the nuts are cool enough to handle, peel off their shells, put them in the saucepan, cover with water, place over medium heat, boil for 20 minutes, and drain. When the nuts are cool enough to handle, chop and place them in the mixing bowl. Meanwhile, melt butter in the small saucepan, and cook onions and celery until the onions are soft and translucent. Mix salt and herbs together in a cup. Add bread to the mixing bowl, and *toss* with the herb mixture. Mix in cooked vegetables and beaten egg. Wash the chicken (inside and outside), and lightly stuff with chestnut mixture. Pull the skin on the chicken breast away from the bird, place fresh herbs there if desired, and replace skin. Lightly sprinkle chicken with salt and pepper, place in roasting pan, insert meat thermometer into chicken thigh, and bake for 30 minutes. Spread a couple tablespoons of sour cream on chicken, and continue roasting for 1½ more hours (until thermometer reaches 180° Fahrenheit), basting with sour cream every 30 minutes. Serve the meat juices with chicken and stuffing. If desired, add water and a little flour or cornstarch to the meat juices to thicken the gravy. Add salt and pepper to taste.

Amish Food History

Huge native chestnut trees were once common from New England to the Carolinas. Imagine picking up fallen nuts under a tree that is as tall as a ten-story building! The trunks of these impressive native trees could be twenty feet in diameter. At one time, one out of every four trees in the Appalachians was a chestnut. Like other immigrants, the Amish and Mennonites enjoyed these flavorful nuts. An Asian fungus attacked the American chestnut tree in 1904 and virtually wiped out this magnificent tree in only thirty-five years.

Maple-Baked Beans

Baked beans are as popular among Mennonite and Amish families as they are in many cultures. Some farm families have sugar maple trees on their property and make their own maple syrup each spring. As with the descendants of other German immigrants, pork features prominently in many meals. If you'd like a vegetarian version of this dish, simply eliminate the meat.

Ingredients:

2 cups dry navy beans
1 cup ham, ¼ pound bacon, or ¼ pound salt pork
*1 medium onion, **diced***
¼ cup brown sugar
¼ cup maple syrup
1 teaspoon dry mustard
1 teaspoon salt
¼ teaspoon pepper
2 cups tomato juice

Cooking utensils you'll need:
stockpot
measuring cups
measuring spoons
baking pan with cover

Directions:

Wash beans, remove any small stones or debris, place in stockpot, cover with water, and let soak overnight. The next day, drain beans, cover with fresh water, and *simmer* for about 2 hours (until tender), adding more water if necessary while cooking. Drain beans but save liquid. Preheat oven to 325° Fahrenheit. Mix beans with remaining ingredients in baking pan. Add reserved water if it seems a little dry, cover, and bake for 3 hours, adding more reserved water and fresh water, as necessary.

Tip:

Some people cook beans in the water that remains after soaking them overnight because they wish to retain any nutrients that have leached into the water. Other people feel the beans are more easily digested if this water is replaced with fresh water.

Amish Culture

November and December are the traditional months for weddings in Amish communities. This most likely developed because of the natural farming cycle dictated by climate. November and December are the least busy times of the farming year, so more time can be devoted to wedding preparations, including cooking the feast. Most Amish weddings take place on either a Tuesday or Thursday. The fact that Sunday is a day of rest makes it impossible to hold weddings on that day or on Saturday (because you would have to clean up on Sunday after the wedding) or Monday (because you would have to prepare for the wedding on Sunday). Weddings are not held on Friday, because it is the day Jesus died, nor on Wednesday, because it is the day Judas betrayed Him.

Two (sometimes three) meals are prepared for a wedding feast. The first is served immediately after the ceremony and lasts for several hours while people are socializing and occasionally singing hymns. A second meal is served in the early evening before gifts are opened. A third meal may be served before guests return to their own homes.

Brown Bread

Amish and Mennonite women are accomplished bakers, and bread is served at every meal. Although white bread is more commonly made, women also bake other types such as this whole-wheat version. This Amish recipe will make 2 delicious and healthy loaves.

Cooking utensils you'll need:
measuring cups
measuring spoons
large mixing bowl
wooden spoon
breadboard
clean dish towel
2 loaf pans

Ingredients:

2 cups very warm water
1 package active dry yeast
1 teaspoon salt
¼ cup softened butter
¼ cup honey
2 tablespoons molasses
3 cups whole-wheat flour
2 cups white flour
cooking oil

Directions:

Pour yeast over very warm water in mixing bowl, and stir to dissolve. Stir in salt, butter, molasses, and honey, and mix well. Stir in whole-wheat flour. Stir in 1 cup of white flour. Continue to stir in as much of the white flour as possible, then sprinkle some of the flour on the bread board and *knead* the dough, adding more flour as necessary. Oil the mixing bowl, place the dough back in the bowl, swish it around to oil the bottom side, and then turn the dough over so the oiled side is on top. Cover the bowl with a towel, and place it in a warm spot until the dough doubles in size. (This will probably take about 1 hour.) Preheat oven to 375° Fahrenheit. Oil your hands, and punch the dough down. Let the dough rest while you oil the loaf pans and the breadboard.

Place half the dough on the board, form it into a loaf, and place it in a loaf pan. Repeat with the second loaf, and bake for 35 or 40 minutes (until loaves are nicely browned and sound hollow when tapped).

Tip:

Turn one of your loaves into cinnamon-raisin bread by forming it into a loaf in the following way: Roll the dough into a rectangle, sprinkle with brown sugar, cinnamon, and raisins, roll up the rectangle. Pinch the seam closed and place it on the bottom. Take some of the dough on the top edges, pull it down over the rolled edges, and tuck it under the loaf.

Amish and Mennonite Culture

Wheat has always been plentiful and economical in rural Amish and Mennonite communities. Perhaps that is one reason why baked goods are so plentiful. The threshing of wheat still occurs on Amish farms in much the same manner as in the past, with machinery and men moving from one farm to another to accomplish this task.

For the Old Order Mennonite and Amish, farming is a way of life that has not changed much over the centuries. Many Amish farmers still use horses and mules rather than tractors, and all farmers work from dawn to dusk, or even longer. Amish families usually include many children, and much food is required to keep energy levels and spirits elevated throughout the day. When an Amish couple becomes elderly, the farm is usually given to one of their sons, and a smaller house, sometimes called a *gossdawdy* house, is often built for the older couple.

Urbanization and the high cost of land make it increasingly difficult for Amish families to continue the farming tradition. This is also true for other farm families.

Corn Chowder

The Amish do not usually serve soups during the main meal of the day, but they are a favorite way to provide nourishment during the remaining meals. They are popular because they utilize available ingredients from the garden and require only stovetop cooking. In Amish homes, soup spoons and other eating utensils are placed to the right of the bowl or plate.

Ingredients:

2 slices of bacon or salt pork
1 medium onion, **diced**
½ cup diced celery
2 medium to large potatoes, diced
2 cups corn cut off the cob (see "Tips")

6 soda crackers
2 cups milk
2 cups chicken broth
¼ teaspoon pepper
salt to taste

Cooking utensils you'll need:
measuring cups
measuring spoons
small bowl
stockpot

Directions:

Cut bacon or salt port into ½- to 1-inch pieces, put it in the stockpot, and cook over medium heat until fat begins to melt out of the meat. Stir in the onion and celery, and cook until the meat is crisp. Stir in potatoes, corn, and chicken broth, and *simmer* until potatoes are tender (15 to 20 minutes). Meanwhile, soak crackers in 1 cup of milk. When potatoes are cooked, add the cracker mixture, remaining 1 cup milk, pepper, and salt to taste. Continue cooking until heated through, stirring occasionally. Serve hot.

Tips:

It's easy to make a vegetarian version of this soup by substituting butter for the bacon or salt pork and water for the chicken broth.

To cut corn off the cob, hold it upright and steady with the stem side down. With a sharp knife in your other hand, slice downward, cutting off a few rows of corn kernels. Then go back and gently scrape that area of the cob to get more of the corn juice. Some people like to place the cob in the center tube of an angel-food cake pan so the cut kernels fall into the pan. You still need to hold the cob steady as you cut when using this method. If fresh corn is not available, use canned whole-kernel corn.

Amish and Mennonite Food History

American Indians were cultivating corn long before the arrival of European immigrants. Amish and Mennonite women were quick to adopt native foods into their own cooking traditions.

You may be surprised to discover that stewed, steamed, and fried saltine crackers soaked in milk are a traditional Amish food. This practice may have started as a means of providing inexpensive meals during the Great Depression. Sometimes fried eggs or other ingredients are added to the cooked crackers before serving.

Rivvels

Add this simple alternative to noodles to chicken stock, beef broth, or any meat- or milk-based soup.

Ingredients:

1 cup flour
salt
1 egg
milk
canned or homemade chicken stock or beef stock

Cooking utensils you'll need:
measuring cup
mixing bowl
pastry blender or fork

Directions:

Put the flour in the mixing bowl and add a couple shakes of salt. *Cut* in the egg. Cut in milk a tablespoon at a time until the mixture is crumbly. Use your hands to crumble little pieces of dough into boiling stock. Pieces can vary between the size of rice and the size of cherry pits. *Simmer* for 10 or 15 minutes.

Amish Food Culture

Knepp is a word used to describe small flour dumplings. Like rivvels, they are sometimes cooked in meat stock or with water and vegetables such as peas. It's easy to make knepp. Just add 1 cup flour, 1 teaspoon baking powder, and 2 teaspoons melted butter to the rivvel recipe. Mix the butter with the egg and ½ cup milk before adding it to the flour mixture, and increase salt to ½ teaspoon. Drop heaping teaspoons of dough into broth or water, simmer 15 minutes, cover, simmer another 10 minutes, and serve.

Amish Culture

Amish communities are thriving. There are close to 100,000 Amish people today. The largest Old Order Amish community in the United States is located in Holmes County, Ohio. The second largest lives in Lancaster County, Pennsylvania. When Amish people move to new areas, they often do so as a group.

Layered Salad

In the past, applesauce was served at many meals as a substitute for salad, especially during winter. Nowadays, salad ingredients are more available and popular. This common make-ahead salad is large enough for a small crowd. Mennonite and Amish families enjoy many salads made with fresh ingredients from the garden. During the winter, more cabbage and potato salads are served.

Ingredients:

1 head iceberg lettuce (or other lettuce)
1 cup celery, **diced**
2 cups fresh or frozen peas
4 eggs
½ cup diced green pepper
1 onion, thinly sliced
1½ to 2 cups mayonnaise
2 tablespoons sugar
2 cups shredded mild or medium cheddar cheese
½ pound bacon

Cooking utensils you'll need:
saucepan
measuring cups
small mixing bowl
9x13-inch glass cake pan
or glass bowl
plastic wrap
skillet

Directions:

Place eggs in cold water in saucepan, place over medium heat, boil 5 minutes, drain, place in cold water, and (when cool enough to handle) peel and slice. Layer first 6 ingredients in the order listed. Mix sugar into mayonnaise, and spread over salad. Sprinkle with cheese, cover with plastic wrap, and refrigerate overnight. The next day, cook bacon in skillet until crisp, drain on paper towels to remove some of the fat, and crumble over salad before serving.

Broccoli Salad

Ingredients:

½ pound bacon (optional)
1 large bunch of broccoli
1 medium onion, very thinly sliced (a red onion is best)
1 cup mayonnaise
2 tablespoons cider vinegar
½ cup sugar
1 cup shredded mild cheddar cheese
½ cup raisins
½ cup chopped walnuts

Cooking utensils you'll need:
skillet
measuring cups
measuring spoon
cheese shredder
mixing bowl

Directions:

Cook bacon until crisp, and place on paper towels to drain off some of the fat. Wash broccoli well, cut into bite-sized pieces, and set aside. Mix mayonnaise, vinegar, and sugar. *Toss* with broccoli, cheese, raisins, nuts, and crumbled bacon, and chill at least 1 hour. Stir, and sprinkle with additional cheese before serving.

Amish and Mennonite Culture

These groups' objection to fighting and war reaches back to the Amish and Mennonite's Anabaptist origins. Early Anabaptists were sometimes tortured and put to death because of their beliefs. During the Revolutionary War in 1776, a group of Amish men in Pennsylvania almost met the same fate. They were arrested, tried, and sentenced to death after refusing to fight against England. They were eventually set free, however, when a minister for the German Reformed Church argued on their behalf, explaining that they had come to the New World seeking religious freedom and that it was not right to expect them to go against their faith. The Federal Conscription Act of 1863 made it possible for men to avoid being drafted during the Civil War by paying $300. This was a large sum, especially for farmers, but Amish communities worked together to raise the necessary money.

Apple Dumplings

Apples are featured in countless Amish and Mennonite dishes. They are used fresh, made into sauce and apple butter, dried (called schnitz), and made into cider and cider vinegar. Apple dumplings are served as a substantial dessert after a light meal or, perhaps even more often, as a meal itself.

Preheat oven to 350° Fahrenheit.

Ingredients:

5 apples	5 tablespoons white sugar
2 cups flour	1¼ teaspoons cinnamon
4 teaspoons baking powder	3 tablespoons butter
½ teaspoon salt	1½ cups water
4 tablespoons shortening	1 cup brown sugar, packed
1 cup milk	light cream (half and half)

Cooking utensils you'll need:
measuring cups
measuring spoons
mixing bowl
pastry blender or 2 knives
rolling pin
breadboard (optional)
saucepan
baking dish

Directions:

Peel and core apples. Stir together flour, baking powder, and salt in mixing bowl. *Cut* in shortening first, and then milk. Divide dough into 5 equal-sized pieces. Sprinkle extra flour on breadboard and rolling pin. Roll out one piece of dough. (Try to roll it into a square.) Place an apple in the center of the dough. Put 1 tablespoon sugar and ¼ teaspoon cinnamon in the apple-core cavity. Bring 2 opposite corners of the dough up over the apple, and pinch them together at the top. Bring one of the remaining corners up to the top of the apple, and pinch its sides closed along the edges of the pieces brought up to the center previously. Repeat with the remaining corner. (Use water like paste to help stick the sides together, if necessary.) Place the apple dumpling in the baking dish, and repeat with the remaining dough and apples. Put the butter, water, and brown sugar in saucepan, and bring to a boil over medium heat. Pour around dumplings, and bake for 40 to 50 minutes (until golden brown).

Amish and Mennonite Food Culture

Amish and Mennonite farm families make many types of pickled vegetables as a means of preserving food for winter. Chow chow is a traditional mixture of several different vegetables preserved in vinegar and sugar. Corn, cabbage, string beans, lima beans, celery, onions, peppers, and cucumbers may all be included in this food that is usually made near the end of the growing season. Although cabbages last for a long time, turning them into sauerkraut is one way to preserve them even longer. Sauerkraut and apples are traditional accompaniments to pork. Many fruits are also canned for winter use and are often turned into delectable desserts. Pickled food and desserts are served on a daily basis in Old Order Amish and Mennonite homes. When guests are present, many pickles and several choices of dessert may be served. According to one saying, these homes serve seven sweets and seven sours. However, it is not routine for this many pickles and desserts to be served at a family meal.

Bread Pudding

Bread that has not been eaten before the new loaves are baked is perfect when made into this old-fashioned dessert.

Preheat oven to 350° Fahrenheit.

Ingredients:

6 tablespoons butter
4 cups milk
1 cup sugar
4 eggs
dash of salt
1 teaspoon vanilla
4 cups bread cut in cubes (1-inch or smaller)
½ cup raisins
cinnamon (optional)
light cream (half and half) or milk

Cooking utensil you'll need:
measuring cups
measuring spoons
whisk
mixing bowl
saucepan
baking dish
larger baking dish

Directions:

Grease the smaller of the two baking dishes with butter, and put the remaining butter in the saucepan with milk and sugar. Place over medium heat, stirring occasionally, until butter is melted. **Whisk** eggs in mixing bowl, and add hot milk slowly while whisking constantly. Stir in vanilla and salt. Place bread cubes in buttered baking dish, and sprinkle with raisins. Pour milk over bread cubes and stir. Sprinkle bread pudding with cinnamon, if desired. Place the smaller baking dish in the larger baking dish. Pour hot water in the larger dish until it goes half way up the smaller dish. Set both dishes in the oven, and bake for 1 hour (until pudding is **set**). Serve with light cream or milk poured over each serving.

Amish Culture

In the 1960s, several Amish families moved from Arkansas and Pennsylvania to Belize. A year later a group from Indiana moved to Paraguay, where several families from Ontario, Canada, later joined them.

Shoofly Pie

Amish and Mennonite pies are legendary and are baked at least weekly in most homes. This dessert is famous among the Pennsylvania Dutch, but for many people its sweetness is an acquired taste. You may want to accompany your first piece of shoofly pie with a scoop of vanilla ice cream and a cup of warm tea.

Preheat oven to 400° Fahrenheit.

Cooking utensils you'll need:
measuring cups
measuring spoons
mixing bowl
pastry blender or 2 butter knives
rolling pin
breadboard or other flat surface
pie pan
small bowl
whisk
saucepan

Ingredients:

1¾ cups flour
salt
⅓ cup plus 2 tablespoons shortening
1 tablespoon butter
milk
½ teaspoon cinnamon
pinch of nutmeg
pinch of cloves

pinch of ginger
½ cup brown sugar, packed
½ tablespoons baking soda
¾ cup water
½ cup molasses
1 egg
vanilla ice cream

Directions:

Place 1 cup flour and ¼ teaspoon salt in mixing bowl, and *cut* in ⅓ cup shortening and the butter. Add milk 1 tablespoon at a time until the dough is firm but sticks together, and place in refrigerator for 10 minutes. Sprinkle flour on breadboard and rolling pin, roll dough, and place it in the pie pan.

Mix ¾ cup flour, cinnamon, nutmeg, cloves, ginger, brown sugar, and a couple shakes of salt. Cut in 2 tablespoons shortening to complete the crumb mixture.

Whisk the egg in the small bowl, and set it aside. Place water in saucepan over medium heat, bring to a boil, and remove from heat. Stir in baking soda, molasses, and egg to complete the molasses mixture. Place alternating layers of crumb mixture and molasses mixture into the pie pan, ending with a crumb layer. Bake for about 15 minutes, turn heat down to 350° Fahrenheit, and continue baking for 20 minutes (until *set*). Let cool and serve with a scoop of vanilla ice cream.

Amish Food History

The Pennsylvania Dutch are famous for making shoofly pie, a sweet molasses-based dessert. Surprisingly, it may have been first served for breakfast. The public was introduced to shoofly pie at the Philadelphia Centennial in 1876, where it was called centennial cake. Some people think it received its present name because of the need to shoo flies away from the sweet confection. Other people think it may be the Americanization of the French word *choufleur*, which is the word for cauliflower. The theory is that the crumbly top layer may have reminded people of this vegetable. The fact that early Amish people did live in France makes this origin seem possible. However, there was also a brand of molasses named "Shoofly" that was originally used in the recipe. The food may have been named after this essential ingredient.

Rhubarb Crunch

Rhubarb is one of the first foods to emerge from the ground in spring—and this old-fashioned perennial is popular for many Mennonite and Amish dishes. Watch for its long celery-like stalks in your supermarket, and use them to make this cake-like dessert.

Ingredients:

1 cup flour
¾ cup uncooked oatmeal (quick-cooking or old fashioned)
1 cup brown sugar, packed
1 teaspoon cinnamon
½ cup melted butter
3 cups rhubarb, *diced*
1 cup sugar
2 tablespoons cornstarch
1 cup water
1 teaspoon vanilla
heavy cream whipped with 1 tablespoon confectioners' sugar (powdered sugar) or vanilla ice cream

Cooking utensils you'll need:
measuring cups
measuring spoons
mixing bowl
saucepan
9x9-inch baking dish

Directions:

Mix the first 5 ingredients together until crumbly, and divide mixture in half. Press one half of the mixture onto the bottom of the baking dish. Meanwhile, mix sugar and cornstarch in the saucepan, stir in water, bring to boil over medium heat, cook and stir until thick, remove from heat, stir in vanilla and rhubarb, and pour mixture into baking dish. Cover with remaining crumbs, and bake for 1 hour. Serve warm or cold with a *dollop* of whipped cream or vanilla ice cream.

Tips:

Substitute apples for 1½ cups of rhubarb to make a mixed-fruit dessert.

Use care when whipping cream because over beating will quickly turn cream into buttermilk and little chunks of butter.

Amish Food History

Rhubarb is sometimes called pie plant because that is how it is usually used. This vegetable was brought to America from Europe sometime between 1790 and 1800. It was available in produce markets in many areas by 1822.

Snickerdoodles

This specialty of the Pennsylvania Dutch is crispy on the outside but moist and chewy on the inside. The old-fashioned cookie with German roots has really stood the test of time. Bake a batch and have a snack that is very similar to one eaten by children in colonial times.

Preheat oven to 400° Fahrenheit.

Ingredients:

1½ cups plus 1 tablespoon sugar
½ cup shortening
½ cup butter
2 eggs
2¾ cups flour
1 teaspoon baking soda
2 teaspoons cream of tartar
¼ teaspoon salt
1 teaspoon cinnamon

Cooking utensils you'll need:
measuring cups
measuring spoons
flour sifter or wire strainer
2 mixing bowls
1 small, shallow bowl
cookie sheet

Directions:

Cream 1½ cups sugar with shortening and butter, stir in eggs one at a time, beating well after each one. Sift flour, baking soda, cream of tartar, and salt into the second bowl, stir, and mix into creamed butter mixture. Mix the remaining tablespoon of sugar and cinnamon in the small bowl. Use your hands to shape cookie dough into small balls (about the size of a walnut), roll the top of the cookies in the sugar/cinnamon mixture, place cinnamon-side-up on cookie sheet, and bake 10 minutes.

Amish and Mennonite Culture

Mennonites build churches where they meet for services, but the Amish do not have an established and formal ministry. Instead, a male member of the community is chosen by lot to serve in this position. Weekly or biweekly church services are held in Amish homes and rotate to various homes throughout the community. Moving the place of worship was one way the Amish avoided religious persecution in Europe during the eighteenth century. German is still used for church services, which last for about three hours. Having church in each other's homes provides an opportunity for the woman in the household to prepare favorite recipes. Pride is a sin in the Amish religion, but women enjoy serving delicious food to family and friends. Many desserts may be served at such events, including cookies such as snickerdoodles.

Amish and Mennonite Culture

The Amish do adopt some new items into their life. While most do not use electricity in their home, for example, many do have refrigerators that operate on propane gas. Telephones are sometimes used for business purposes, or a family member may borrow a neighbor's phone to make a doctor's appointment. On the other hand, most traditions are firmly held and have helped to preserve the Amish way of life.

Popcorn Surprise "Cake"

You may not associate a whimsical food like this with Amish and Mennonite families, but birthdays are cause for celebration in these homes just as they are in your own. This fun food is sometimes served at such events.

Ingredients:

12 cups popped popcorn
peanuts (as many as you like)
¼ cup plus 2 tablespoons butter
one 10½-ounce bag miniature marshmallows
1 teaspoon vanilla
M&M's® (as many as you like)

Cooking utensils you'll need:
measuring cup
measuring spoons
mixing bowl
large sauce pan
angel food cake pan
buttered rubber spatula

Directions:

Butter the angel food cake pan and spatula. Put the popcorn and peanuts in the mixing bowl. Melt butter in saucepan over low heat, stir in marshmallows, continue stirring until melted, pour over popcorn and peanuts, and stir. Mix in M&M's, and press mixture into buttered cake pan. The buttered spatula may help you get all of the mixture out of the bowl and press it into the pan, but use your hands when necessary. Let the cake rest at least 1 hour before unmolding. Allow everyone to pull the cake apart to eat it, or cut it into serving pieces.

Further Reading

Adams, Marcia. *New Recipes from Quilt Country: More Food & Folkways from the Amish & Mennonites*. New York: Clarkson N. Potter, 1997.

Coleman, Bill. *The Gift to Be Simple: Life in Amish Country*. San Francisco, Calif.: Chronicle Books LLC, 2001.

Good, Merl. *An Amish Portrait: Song of a People*. Intercourse, Pa.: Good Books, 1997.

Herr, Patricia T. *Amish Quilts of Lancaster County*. Atglen, Pa.: Schiffer Publishing, Ltd., 2004.

Igou, Brad. *The Amish in Their Own Words: Amish Writings from 25 Years of Family Life Magazine*. Danvers, Mass.: Herald Press, 1999.

Pellman Good, Phyllis. *The Best of Amish Cooking*. Intercourse, Pa.: Good Books, 1996.

Pellman Good, Phyllis, and Rachel Thomas Pellman. *From Amish and Mennonite Kitchens*. Intercourse, Pa.: Good Books, 1998.

Shank, Esther H. *Mennonite Country-Style Recipes and Kitchen Secrets*. New York: Gramercy Books, 2000.

Stewart, Jillian, ed. *Amish Cooking*. Philadelphia, Pa.: Courage Books, 1995.

Williams, Kevin, and Elizabeth Coblentz. *The Amish Cook: Recollections and Recipes from an Old Order Amish Family*. Berkeley, Calif.: Ten Speed Press, 2002.

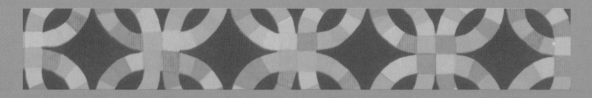

For More Information

Amish History
pittsburgh.about.com/cs/pennsylvania/a/amish.htm

Amish Recipes
www.geocities.com/Heartland/Acres/4207/amish.html
www.nancyskitchen.com/amish.asp

Amish and Mennonite History
www.800padutch.com/amish.shtml

Amish and Mennonite Recipes
www.recipegoldmine.com/regionalamish/amish.html

Questions and Answers about Amish Life
www.amish.net/faq.asp

Sensitively Taken Photos of Amish Life
amishphotos.com

Publisher's note:
The Web sites listed on this page were active at the time of publication. The publisher is not responsible for Web sites that have changed their addresses or discontinued operation since the date of publication. The publisher will review and update the Web sites upon each reprint.

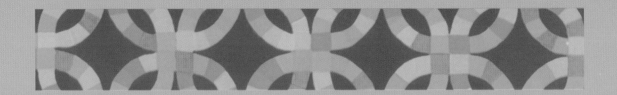

Index

Index

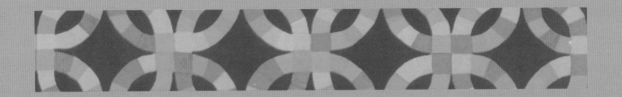

Author:

In addition to writing, Joyce Libal has worked as an editor for a half dozen magazines, including a brief stint as recipe editor at *Vegetarian Gourmet*. Most of her experience as a cook, however, has been gained as the mother of three children and occasional surrogate mother to several children from different countries and cultures. She is an avid gardener and especially enjoys cooking with fresh herbs and vegetables and with the abundant fresh fruit that her husband grows in the family orchard.

Recipe Tester / Food Preparer:

Bonni Phelps owns How Sweet It Is Café in Vestal, New York. Her love of cooking and feeding large crowds comes from her grandmothers on both sides whom also took great pleasure in large family gatherings.

Consultant:

The Culinary Institute of America is considered the world's premier culinary college. It is a private, not-for-profit learning institution, dedicated to providing the world's best culinary education. Its campuses in New York and California provide learning environments that focus on excellence, leadership, professionalism, ethics, and respect for diversity. The institute embodies a passion for food with first-class cooking expertise.

Picture Credits

Concept Images: p. 9; Corbis: cover, pp. 12, 53, 68, 69; Dover: cover; PhotoDisc: cover; Photos.com: pp. 15, 16, 18, 23, 26, 28, 33, 37, 38, 40, 50, 68, 69; Benjamin Stewart: pp. 15, 16, 18, 21, 24, 35, 43, 44, 46, 49, 55, 56, 60, 63, 64; Ron Wilson Photography: pp. 10, 19, 31, 68, 69